I0540564

Love Letters

Shannon Beardsmore

The opinions expressed in this publication are the author's own. This publication is sold with the understanding that the author and publisher are not engaged in rendering psychological, financial, or other professional services. If expert advice or counseling is needed, the reader is encouraged to consult a professional.

978-1-968944-05-6

Copyright © 2026 Soul Sparks Press. All Rights Reserved. No part of this publication may be reproduced, distributed, or transmitted in any form or by any means, including photocopying, recording, or other electronic or mechanical methods, without the prior written permission of the publisher, except in the case of brief quotations embodied in critical reviews and certain other noncommercial uses permitted by copyright law. For permission requests, please contact the publisher at soulsparkspress.com.

This
journal
belongs to

_____

To my beautiful dreamers,

This journal is a lighthouse for your heart. If you are holding it, it is because something inside of you is ready to be seen, heard, and loved. You didn't stumble here. You were guided.

This journal is for the soul that carries everyone yet still imagines for themselves. For the soul who had their heart shattered and knows their true love is still out there. For the soul who feels their dreams are too big but can't deny the spark that keeps lighting up inside of her.

These pages are to help you remember all of you. Your heart, your dreams, your desires. Your life is meant to be lived full out, and no matter where your life is today, it is all perfectly timed. You are the person your younger self prayed for, right now, page by page, tear by tear, choice by choice.

This journal is my gift to you. I hope my shanny-isms inspire you to write love letters to yourself, and as you do choose you each and every moment of each and every day. May every letter you write to yourself help you remember the most beautiful, important, and loving person in your world is YOU.

I pray you experience all the love, clarity, and magic throughout these pages and inside of YOU!

With so much love and light.

love

—Shanny

How to use
this journal

♥ Write when your heart is heavy. Pour it out. Spill everything onto these pages. Release, release, release.

♥ Write when your heart is glowing. Celebrate yourself. Capture you. Love on this journey.

♥ Write when you feel too busy, too tired, too stretched, and even the days when you feel not enough. It is in those moments when the magic unlocks. When you pause to reconnect with yourself, you connect with your inner source.

♥ Let these letters be your mirror. As you write, you'll start to see your strength, your softness, your grit, your desires. You'll see the woman you're becoming.

♥ Please let it be messy. Let it be honest. There is no wrong way to show up here. If it comes from your heart, it belongs.

♥ Come back to it as often as you need. Daily, weekly, whenever your soul knocks. There is no right or wrong way to journal. Some days it might just be one word and that is perfectly okay.

♥ Inside you is a mustard seed of desire so powerful, so divinely planted, that even on the loud, crowded days it keeps whispering, "I'm here. You've got this." These pages are to give that whisper a space to be heard.

GO HAVE
a napitation ♥

A napitation is the best kind of happy accident. When you sit down to meditate, get cozy, and whoops... drift off into the sweetest little nap.

Guess what? Your body and soul still soak up all that good, healing energy. Whether you're meditating or napping, you're giving yourself love, and that's always a win!

Love to love to love ya! ♡

I love me

SELF LOVE

is not selfish
it's necessary ♥

You can't pour from an empty cup.
Loving yourself is an act of grace.
When you can love yourself deeply,
you create space to love others fully.
Permission for people to love you
back. Self love is the foundation of
everything.

If it's easy it's from God

I love me

JESUS IS
my homeboy ♥

I have a relationship with my
creator and it's fun. Period!

I love me so much I give
myself high 5's every morning

I love me

THIS ISN'T
happening to you
it's happening
for you ♥

Every experience, every moment, and every shift in your life is a divine opportunity for growth and alignment with your highest self.

Life isn't working against you; it's working with you, guiding you gently toward your purpose. Even when things feel uncertain, trust that everything is unfolding for your highest good, helping you step into the love and wisdom that's always been within you.

I love me

Every challenge I face is an
opportunity to love myself more deeply

I AM F♥CKING
proud of me ♥

A gentle, loving acknowledgment of your persistence and strength. It's celebrating the growth, the grace, and the courage it took to keep moving forward, even when things weren't easy. It's recognizing the love you've nurtured for yourself, the resilience you've shown, and the beauty in your journey. This is your heart speaking, honoring the love and peace you've cultivated within, knowing that every step forward is worthy of celebration.
You're f♥cking awesome!

I choose to love myself
today no matter what

I love me

WHO SITS
at your table ♥

Selecting who sits at your table is a deliberate and empowering choice of self worth. It influences your life's direction. It can either empower you or disable you.

God is my CEO

I love me

GO SNIFF
a tree ♥

Translation: Get out of your head and back into your heart.

Touch the earth. Breathe in the moment.
Let God speak to you through his world – the wind, the bark, the birds, the stillness.

When the world gets loud, go sniff a tree.

Let nature reset your nervous system and remind you: You are held, you are here, and you are part of something way bigger.

I love me

BE YOUR OWN
best friend ♥

Hype yourself. Love on yourself. Take yourself on dates, talk yourself up in the mirror, and laugh at your own jokes.
Talk to yourself like someone you're madly in love with.

I am open to receive all the love ♡

I love me

I CELEBRATE
the depth of my
own heart ♥

I celebrate the places no one sees but me and God. The quiet strength, the fire, the vulnerability. I honor the woman I was who is now aware of the women I am today.

The more I love me, the
more I love the world

I love me

MAKE THIS
healing fun ♥

Put on your favorite song and dance.
Go for a walk and sit on the juiciest
grass. Whatever makes you smile, do
that and more of it.

You were made for MORE. More
FUN. More LOVE. More LIFE.

I love me

WHEN YOU TRULY
love yourself,
that is freedom ♥

When you truly love yourself, that's where freedom begins. No more chasing, no more shrinking. Just a deep, steady peace in knowing you are already enough. Every choice, every boundary, every breath becomes an act of devotion. That's soul liberation.

I am worthy of my own
love and compassion

I love me

YOUR
thoughts are the
BLUEPRINT
of your reality ♥

Every belief you hold (good or bad), every story you repeat, lays the foundation for what you experience. Whatever your mind is aligned with must happen. Whether it is love or fear. Your choice is to see what you're thinking because what you are thinking becomes your reality.

Let God be the filter

I love me

YOUR ENERGY
is precious ♥

Please don't waste it proving,
pleasing, or explaining it to
anyone.

Some friendships feel
like coming home

I love me

LEAP INTO
the unknown ♥

Trusting love instead of fear.
Letting go of control.
Choosing faith over certainty.
It's where miracles happen.

The scariest thing you can imagine is
the very thing you must do to grow

I love me

NOTHING
is real ♥

Nothing is real. It's all a matter of perception. Reality shifts with the lens through which we view it. What we experience is shaped by our thoughts, beliefs, and emotions.

What seems heavy and hard can be light and liberating when seen through the eyes of love.

Listen to the whisper

I love me

DESTINED
to be ME! ♥

It's a beautiful knowing that my soul's purpose is already within me, waiting to unfold. When I listen to my God compass, I align with the divine guidance that leads me toward my highest self.

A mindset so disciplined I
knew it was coming

I love me

SELF CARE
is my flex ♥

I do activities that nourish my body, mind, and spirit, embracing practices that make me feel fabulous. By filling my own cup, I not only enhance my happiness but also inspire those around me to do the same, creating a ripple effect of positivity and self love.

Let God guide the glow

I love me

I AM IN LOVE

with all of me ❤

I am in love with ALL OF ME!
The wild. The soft. The loud. The too
much. The not enough. The healed parts
and the messy middle.
ALL OF IT. Every flavor. Every phase.
Every "Omg girl, we really did that?"
moment.

I'm fully obsessed. Head over heels.
Best friend energy with my own damn
heart. THIS is the love story I've been
waiting for.

GRATEFUL ♡

I love me

BE THE
lighthouse ♡

When you heal and share your story,
you remind others they're not alone.
That's when your light grows even
bigger, illuminating the path for all
who need hope and healing. Keep
shining your beautiful light.

It's not who you are becoming. It's
remembering who the F you are

I love me

TAKE
the fog off
your eyes ♥

Removing the illusions, fears, and false beliefs that keep you from seeing clearly.

It's the shift from fear to love, from separation to connection. When the fog lifts, you remember the truth: you are whole, you are light, and everything real is rooted in love.

Love is supposed to feel light ♡

I love me

GROWTH

doesn't come

from staying

comfortable ♥

Oh babe, comfort keeps you cozy—
but stuck.

Growth... she lives on the edge of
discomfort, in the stretch, the
sweat, in the "WTF am I doing?"
moments.

If you're not being stretched,
you're not being shaped. So quit
playing small and lean into the
fire. That's where the magic is.

I love the love I am giving myself

I love me

GET FACE
to face with
your fears ♥

Look your fear dead in the eye.
Don't run. Don't shrink.
Take your power back.
Boldly confront what's been holding
you back and show it who's boss.

You need friends who
hold a flashlight

I love me

YOU ARE THE
best gift God
has given you ♥

No one else on this planet shines
quite like you.

You're a one of a kind masterpiece,
wrapped in grace, strength, and
fierce magic.

I love me

GRATITUDE
is the heart ♥

The heartbeat of presence, love, and alignment. It's the soul's way of saying yes to the now.

When you lead with gratitude, you soften, you expand, you attract more of what's true and beautiful. It's not just a feeling... It's a frequency that brings you back home to yourself.

It's okay to shake
yourself to your core

I love me

LOVE IS IN

every small

act of care ♥

Although the big breakthroughs are powerful, the real transformation is in the little things you do for you. Sipping that water when you don't feel like it. Going for a walk when you'd rather scroll. Pausing to breathe instead of powering through. Letting yourself rest without the shame. Looking in the mirror with love, not critique.

It's in those quiet, ordinary moments you choose yourself over and over. That's not selfish, that's divine.

Choosing what is best for your
body is what is best for you

I love me

IT'S THE
thought of the
thought ♥

The thought of the thought is not the first thought you have, but the deeper, subconscious beliefs that follows.

For example, when someone buys a lottery ticket, their first thought might be, "I'll buy one!" But then, the second thought is, "I'm not going to win anyway."

That second thought is what truly shapes their experience. It's the hidden beliefs, the repeated patterns in our minds, that often determine whether we succeed or fall short, not just the initial idea or action.

JOY (Jesus over yourself)

I love me

MAYBE THE
thing you are

avoiding is the

gateway to your

next level ♥

Stop side eyeing that convo, the boundary, the big bold move that you know you need to do. Those steps are the exact gateway to your next level. Face it, feel it, and walk through it like the powerful force you are.

That resistance you feel is just your breakthrough in disguise.

UNDERSTANDING

I love me

I AM HERE
to love ♥

You are here to remember love, choose love and BE love. It's about bringing love to every moment, every thought, every interaction. That's healing. That's your purpose. That's why you're here.

PEACE

I love me

HEALING

is God's love

in action ♥

Healing isn't about fixing, it's about remembering.

Remembering who you are.
Remembering WHOSE you are.
Letting love fill every crack, every scar, every place that forgot it was worthy.

So if you're healing you're not behind. You're not broken.
You're being wrapped in God's gentlest "I got you."

One breath, one layer, one miracle at a time.

Soul Sisters are the lights that
shine the brightest in our lives

I love me

IF IT
triggers you
it's for you ♥

When something shakes you, it's not
here to hurt you, it's a blessing! It's
here to heal you.
Get curious. Ask, "What's this
showing me about me?"

Seeing life through God's lense ♡

I love me

LOVE
your circle ♥

Make sure your circle are people that see your light, protect your peace and celebrate your wins. Your circle should give you belly laughs, soul level safety and trust. It's about being aligned with the right people that see you for your true self.

Let your perspective shift

I love me

STRETCH
my vessel ♥

Expand my capacity to hold truth, beauty, and the goodness of life. Allow me to grow in wisdom, in purpose, in divine energy.

To be stretched in faith, in awareness, in soul beyond my old limits.

Everything and
everyone is connected

I love me

NO SHADE
no shame
no guilt ♥

A state of grace where you no longer carry the weight of blame. It means allowing yourself to grow without punishment, to evolve in peace without dragging your past into your present. It's choosing love over self-judgment, and honoring your healing without apology. It's freedom, softness, and deep acceptance. Just pure love for yourself.

Every step forward is
worthy of celebra

I love me

COLLABORATION
is currency ♥

It's what happens when God brings hearts together! When we co-create with God at the center, miracles become the blueprint. And when people come together in love, in truth, in alignment that is true wealth.

Whatever makes you smile,
do that and more of it

I love me

YOUR

intuition is

God's compass ♥

God's compass is your God given little nudgie.
It's the divine GPS built into your soul.

It doesn't shout, it's a nudge it whispers with wisdom.

It's the knowing that doesn't need proof, the peace that doesn't need permission.

When you follow it, you're not guessing you're partnering with Heaven's plan.

Trust the tug, follow the flow, and let God guide the glow.

Loving yourself is
an act of grace

I love me

DANCING
is my love
language ♥

It's joy in motion.
Medicine wrapped in music.

Self love is the
foundation of everything

I love me

EVERYTHING
is energy ♥

When you know this, things become easier to see and let go of. Every thought, every word, every feeling carries a frequency. Love is the highest one. When you move in love, you align with the truth of the universe. Everything and everyone is connected. ONE LOVE.

No one else on this planet
shines quite like you

I love me

I AM AUTHOR

of my own story

and I choose

TO WRITE

with love ♥

I hold the pen.
I get to rewrite the narrative, flip the script, choose the plot twists, the comeback scenes, and the wild, beautiful dreams. No one else gets to decide who I am or where I'm going. That's my divine assignment.

Choose faith over fear and bless
every step of the journey

I love me

SING!
change your
frequency ♥

Sound shifts energy.
It lifts the heaviness, clears the
fog, and calls your spirit home.

＿＿＿＿ ♥ ＿＿＿＿

Just comfortably in love with myself

I love me

thank
you

Thank you for choosing love. Especially the kind you give yourself. You are seen. You are held. You are guided.

With all my love and light.

-Shanny ♡

Dear Shanny,

You are a living lighthouse.

You help light up the path so people see God within themselves.

Your loving presence and fun help heal, awaken, and ignite the truth within people.

You are all love, fueled by faith, and guided by purpose.
Your soul's purpose is to shine so others can rise.
This is who I am. This is why I'm here.
And today, I walk in love, fully.

The vibe you're putting out heats up or cools down your reality. When you raise your energy, you turn up the heat on your dreams, attracting more warmth, light, and life. Keep your frequency high, and watch your world glow and grow.

The joy and fun you have is the frequency you're going to attract the magic from. Playing in your imagination is how you bring your manifestation to you. Play so big that you have to giggle and ask, how is that going to happen?

love
−Shanny

Scan here to learn
more about

Scan here to learn more
about Shannon Beardsmore

www.ingramcontent.com/pod-product-compliance
Lightning Source LLC
Chambersburg PA
CBHW071714120626

46550CB00001B/232